Gorillas

Gorillas
the greatest apes

Michael Bright

London, New York, Sydney, Dehli, Paris, Munich, and Johannesburg

Publisher: Sean Moore
Editorial director: LaVonne Carlson
Project editor: Barbara Minton
Editor: Jennifer Quasha
Art editor: Gus Yoo
Production director: David Proffit

First published in 2000 by
BBC Worldwide Ltd,
Woodlands, 80 Wood Lane, London W12 0TT

ISBN 0-7894-7154-X

Produced for BBC Worldwide by Toucan Books Ltd, London

Printed and bound in France
by Imprimerie Pollina s.a. - n° 81933-B

Color separations by Imprimerie Pollina s.a.

Contents

GENTLE GIANTS

GENTLE GIANTS

The air is damp, and the mountain forests of the Virunga Mountains are shrouded in mist. Just as the sun breaks through the clouds, a high-pitched sound breaks the stillness. The scream becomes louder, rises in pitch, and then drops lower. Suddenly, the air is shattered by a chorus of screams, and five enormous gorillas bulldoze their way through the foliage. They stand up abruptly and stay still, the hair of their head crests standing erect. Their lips are pulled back, exposing their black, tartar-covered canine teeth, and their normally soft brown eyes glint yellow.

The butt of their aggression is a lone male. He rises on his hindlegs and claps his hands to his chest, but the display is more a way of saving face than an actual serious threat. At the first opportunity, he flees, the screams of the other gorillas echoing in his ears. They stand defiant until all trace of the lone interloper has gone. Then, silently, they file back into the undergrowth.

Previous page: Portrait of a large male western lowland gorilla, one of the great apes and a close living relative of orangutans, chimpanzees, bonobos, and humans.

THE "GORILLAE"

An angry gorilla has a fearsome appearance, and because of tales from early explorers and films such as *King Kong,* made in the 1930s, the animal gained a sinister and frightening reputation. However, unlike many of its primate relatives, such as the mischievous chimpanzee and the wily baboon, the gorilla is a peace loving, family creature and avoids conflict with people. Nevertheless, it is a powerful animal, the world's largest living primate, and when threatened is potentially dangerous. It is also the most vulnerable, since gorillas live in places racked by wars or threatened by deforestation and are targeted by unscrupulous hunters and poachers.

The first record of a gorilla seen by a European was in 470 BC, when a Carthaginian expedition led by Hanno explored the west coast of Africa. These early voyagers brought back tales of "hairy people" or "gorillae", which they described as "some kind of monkey". It was not until many centuries later that more travelers' tales began to filter back to Europe about these powerful creatures.

In 1625 one such tale was told by Andrew Battell, an English seaman from Essex. He described two creatures that lived in the woods of western Africa, a large animal the local people called "Pongo" and a smaller one known as "Engeco," most likely the gorilla and chimpanzee. He wrote, "The Pongo is in all proportion like a man; but that he is more like a giant in stature than a man; for he is tall, and hath a man's face, hollow-eyed, with long haire upon his browes. His face and eares are without haire, and his hands also. His bodie is full of haire, but not thicke; and it is of a dunnish color." Battell went on to describe how the Pongo "fall upon elephants which come to feed where they be, and so beate them with their clubbed fists" and

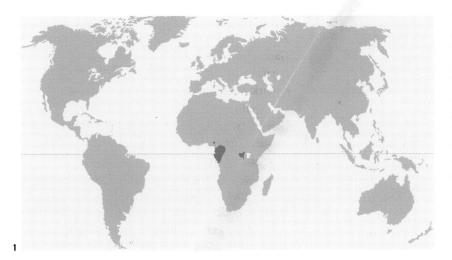

1. Western lowland gorillas, along with chimpanzees and bonobos, inhabit the lowland rain forests of West Africa. In central Africa eastern lowland gorillas live in lowland forests and highland areas, and mountain gorillas live in a region of active volcanoes.

1

★ In order to get as much as possible out of their low-protein, high-fiber diet, gorillas sometimes recycle their food by eating their own dung.

wrote that "those Pongoes are never taken alive because they are so strong, that ten men cannot hold one of them."

Battell's account was not followed with another for over two centuries. In 1819 Thomas Bowdwich wrote in his *Mission from Cape Coast to Ashantee* about "a beast five feet tall and four across at the shoulders." Science, however, was to be denied a formal description for many more years.

Wild man of the woods

Of all the apes, the gorilla was the last to be discovered for science. Nicolaas Tulp of Amsterdam wrote of the chimpanzee in 1641. Jacob Bontius, another Dutchman, described the orangutan in 1658, and a description of the gibbon by French-man Georges Louis Leclerc Compte de Buffon appeared in 1766. The gorilla, however, did not make it into scientific literature until the mid-nineteenth century when Thomas Savage, an American missionary, was visiting what is now Gabon and was shown "a skull, represented by the natives to be that of a monkey-like animal, remarkable for its size, ferocity, and habits".

Together with Jeffrey Wyman of Harvard University, Savage published a paper in the Boston *Journal of Natural History* in 1847. It was based on four skulls, a male, and female pelvis, and some limb bones, ribs, and vertebrae that were shipped back to the US. They were from lowland gorillas, and they could provide information only about the gorilla's anatomy, nothing about its behavior. The prospect of studying animals in the deeply

1. Before gorillas were studied scientifically, they were thought to leap down from trees and throttle passing travelers, as depicted in this 19th-century woodcut.

2. Gorillas were the last of the apes to be described but, having found them, people behaved in the usual way when confronted with newly discovered creatures, they shot them for trophies.

2

unpleasant, mosquito-infested swamps did nothing to encourage nineteenth-century natural historians to record behavior accurately, so they relied on stories from the local people.

The gorilla was called the "wild man of the woods" and was considered to be extremely dangerous. The British zoologist Richard Owen describes how local people traveling through the forest would know that gorillas were around when one of their party was "hoisted up into the tree, uttering, perhaps, a short choking cry. In a few minutes he falls to the ground a strangled corpse." It was also claimed that gorillas, along with chimpanzees, were guilty of capturing young maidens and ravishing them in the forest, stories that gave rise, no doubt, to the infamous King Kong

1. People in some traditional societies are in awe of the gorilla, and parts of its body are considered to have magical properties for use in charms and medicines.

and the wild gorilla's unsavory reputation. In light of these tales, it can be understood why, following the publication of Charles Darwin's *On the Origin of Species* in 1859 and Richard Owen's *Memoir of a Gorilla* in 1865, the prospect of the gorilla being a close relative of humans was greeted with a degree of incredulity.

Field studies

The first attempts at serious field study at the end of the nineteenth century involved naturalists sitting in cages in the forest. Rupert Garner was one of those naturalists. He saw few gorillas, but did describe how an inquisitive five-year-old gorilla stood staring at him with his tongue pushed out between parted lips. The young gorilla was concentrating hard on this strange creature in the forest. Garner was in his cage because these pioneering researchers thought gorillas would attack them. Previously, explorers had embellished their stories to make their own exploits seem more

courageous. Classic among them was Paul du Chaillu, who in the mid-nineteenth century published stories of his travels in West Africa. On seeing a gorilla, he wrote: "He reminded me of some hellish dream creature, a being of that hideous order, half man, half beast," and referring to an adult male, he describes how "one blow of that huge paw, with its bony claws, and the poor hunter's entrails are torn out, his breast bone broken or his skull crushed."

In reality, gorillas avoid people. An adult male might display at an intruder who approaches too close to his group by beating his chest, roaring, and pulling up vegetation. He may charge, but it is mainly bluff. When startled, however, he may attack for real. There is an authenticated case of a gorilla charging and killing a person in 1910, when a member of the Boringo tribe in Uganda happened upon a gorilla family and was attacked by the dominant male. The Boringo man's corpse was found minus his head and neck, which were lying on the ground nearby. This attack was unprovoked and unusual, but since then several hunters and poachers have been killed by large male gorillas after shooting or harming members of their group. Researchers have been on the receiving end of a male gorilla's wrath, too. In 1959, two Japanese workers were tracking a group too closely and the male crashed into one of them and ran him over, crushing his body, and filmmaker Alan Root was charged by a large male when filming the wildlife sequences for the feature film *Gorillas in the Mist*.

It is surprising that gorillas have not been more aggressive toward humankind, because people have mistreated these creatures since their first discovery. Mountain gorillas, for example, were found by Westerners as recently as 1902, when Belgian army officer Captain Oscar von Beringe

came across them in the Virunga Mountains. Confronted with an unknown animal he did what comes naturally to humans. He shot two of them. One fell into a ravine and was lost, while the other was skinned and boned and the pieces were sent back to Europe.

Collectors who were capturing live animals for zoos were no better. Entire families of gorillas were shot in order to take the babies, and many of these died soon after capture. Most have been lowland gorillas, and they have enabled scientists to study biochemistry, evolution, anatomy, and physiology, but little else. There were 661 lowland gorillas in zoos all over the world as of March 2000, but no mountain gorillas in captivity. Curiously, the gorillas you see in zoos are the ones we know least about in the wild.

 PIONEERS OF FIELD RESEARCH

Gorillas avoid people, yet field researchers are able to study them, using techniques pioneered by George Schaller and Dian Fossey. Schaller was the first to observe mountain gorillas in the wild, in 1959 and 1960. His base was Kambara, near Mt. Mikeno in the Congolese section of the Virunga mountains. Inspired by Schaller and the anthropologist Louis Leakey, Fossey went to live with the mountain gorillas at Karisoke in Rwanda's Virunga mountains in 1967. Tragically, she was killed by poachers several years later, but the research station she founded became an important study center at which many of today's gorilla researchers start their careers.

Dian Fossey with gorillas.

FROM THE MOUNTAINS TO THE FOREST

Gorillas live in the wild only in Africa. Some populations inhabit mountain forests and others lowland rain forests. Wherever they are found, they are rare, and because they inhabit dense forests where they are difficult to observe, science has been slow to reveal how they live their every-day lives. Scientists are not even sure how many types of gorillas there are. In April 2000 a conference of primate specialists in Washington, DC recognized two distinct species, the eastern gorilla (*Gorilla berengei*) and the western gorilla (*Gorilla gorilla*), and five subspecies, with a possible new subspecies from Bwindi, Uganda. The differences between them are slight, but new information about anatomy, vocalizations, behavior, and chromosome numbers, as well as the sequencing of their mitochondrial and nuclear DNA, has revealed significant differences. The process of classification of these animals is also ongoing, so further changes can be expected in the future.

The mountain gorilla (*Gorilla berengei berengei*) is found at an altitude of 2100–3650 m in a 728 sq. km patch of mountain forest in the Virunga volcanoes, on the war-torn border between the Parc National des Volcans in northwest Rwanda, the Mgahinga National Park in southwest Uganda, and the Parc National des Virungas in the eastern part of the Democratic Republic of Congo. An isolated population of mountain gorillas in the Bwindi-

1. (opposite) The lowland gorilla has short black hair with brown or reddish tinges on the scalp.

2. The mountain gorilla has long black hair around its face, although it is sparse on the face itself.

2

1

2

1. A dominant male western lowland gorilla shows the silver hair on its back and thighs.

2. The eastern lowland gorilla has longer hair than its western relatives, and appears halfway between the lowland and mountain gorillas.

Impenetrable National Park of Uganda appears to be more closely related to the eastern lowland gorilla, and it is thought it could be a separate subspecies. It has not yet been given a name.

The eastern lowland gorilla (*Gorilla berengei graueri*) lives in the rain forests of eastern Congo, to the west of Lake Tanganyika and Lake Edward, at altitudes of 2500-7400 ft (760–2255 m). It is separated by a 620 mi (1000-km) gap from the western lowland gorilla. The western lowland gorilla is found mainly in Gabon, Equatorial Guinea, western Congo, and the southwestern part of the Central African Republic. A third population of lowland gorillas, known as the Cross River gorilla (*Gorilla gorilla diehli*), is recognized in southeast Nigeria and southern Cameroon. The population was thought to be extinct until news of gorillas in southeast Nigeria was confirmed in 1987. There had been no previous reports for 30 years. Now the Cross River gorillas are considered to be among the most endangered animals on the planet and have been given the conservation status "critically endangered."

The largest of primates

Gorillas are big. A male mountain gorilla that is 5.5 ft (1.7 m) tall when standing upright may have an arm span of 7.5 (2.3 m) and weigh up to 500 lb (227 kg). In comparison, a 5.5 ft (1.7m)-tall adult male human weighs about 154 lb (70 kg). Female gorillas are slightly shorter and less bulky than males.

The male gorilla has massive crests on the top and back of his head. These are areas of   ▷▷

1

1. A group of mountain gorillas sits in its mountain forest home surrounded by food plants. The first feed is often in the morning while still sitting in bed.

2. A group of western lowland gorillas gathers around the dominant male, or silverback, during a rest period between excursions in search of fruit.

★ The parasites found in a mountain gorilla's intestines are closely related to the gut parasites of cattle and antelope, a reflection, perhaps, of their mainly vegetarian diet.

2

thickened bone, the sagittal crest running down the center of the skull and the nuchal crest running across the back of the head. The crests enlarge as a male reaches adulthood and are largest in older dominant males. They are smaller in females. They provide anchoring and support for large muscles, such as the temporal muscles needed to operate the jaws for breaking up plant material.

Gorilla teeth are similar to those of other great apes, but they do not have the flat incisors typical of fruit-eating chimpanzees and orangutans. Their large molars or cheek teeth fracture the huge quantities of vegetation they consume by slicing rather than crushing. This means that gorillas chop their food, like somebody chopping herbs and vegetables on a cutting board.

Most gorillas have black or brown-gray fur with black skin on the chest, palms, and face, although redheads are also relatively common among the Cameroon gorillas. The leading male in a group is known as the "silverback," because he has conspicuous silver-gray fur on his back and thighs. Infants have a white tuft on the rump. Western and eastern lowland gorillas can be distinguished by their noses. The western race has an overhanging tip to its nose. Mountain gorillas differ from their low-land cousins in having longer body hair, higher foreheads, larger nostrils, broader chests, shorter arms and wider hands and feet.

Both male and female gorillas have long arms, short legs, a broad, shallow chest, and short trunk. The long arms indicate a tree-dwelling ancestry. Living gorillas, however, spend most of their time on the ground, although they are capable of shinning up

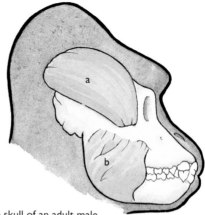

1. The skull of an adult male western gorilla, showing the temporal muscle (a) that makes up the crest and the masseter muscle (b) that works the jaw.

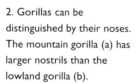

2. Gorillas can be distinguished by their noses. The mountain gorilla (a) has larger nostrils than the lowland gorilla (b).

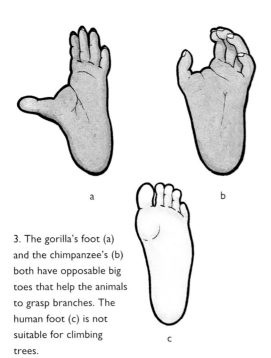

a

b

c

3. The gorilla's foot (a) and the chimpanzee's (b) both have opposable big toes that help the animals to grasp branches. The human foot (c) is not suitable for climbing trees.

a

b

4. Gorillas walk on their knuckles (a), which have a layer of thick skin on the fingers (b) for protection.

a tree in order to reach their favorite fruits. The thumb is much smaller than a human's, and is capable of much more precise manipulation than the larger thumb of the chimpanzee and orangutan. On the foot the big toe is opposable, it is capable of being moved into a position facing the other toes. Therefore a gorilla can grasp a branch with its feet and climb trees with ease, although the number of limb injuries seen on lowland gorillas indicates that they often fall out. Swinging from the arms, like a gibbon, is seen only in young gorillas.

A gorilla usually walks on all fours, with the soles of its feet flat on the ground, with its fists partly clenched, and with its knuckles placed on the ground to support the weight of the forequarters. It has a layer of thick skin on the back of the second joint of each finger to take the wear. The gorilla skeleton has similar components to the human skeleton except that the bones are thicker and the spine lacks the curvature needed for prolonged upright walking. Nevertheless, a gorilla can stand on its two legs and does occasionally, particularly when threatening, displaying, fighting a rival, or playing. It can run bipedally, or on two legs, for about 6 m. It has no tail.

The gorilla differs from the chimpanzee by having small ears that are set close to the head, and the external genitalia are not obvious. Its muzzle is short and without hair; the nostrils are flared, and the jaws are strong. The chinless lower jaw is substantial. The gorilla's small eyes are usually dark brown, and they are protected by a prominent brow ridge. Both sexes have an enormous "pot belly," which accommodates the large intestine needed to digest and absorb the bulky plant food on which the gorilla feeds.

MAINLY VEGETARIAN

Mountain gorillas eat about 200 different species of forest plants, including wild celery, thistles, nettles, wild cherry, wild blackberry, narrow-leafed ferns, and bamboo shoots, but their staple diet appears to be the Gallium vine. They eat flowers, leaves, stems, shoots, roots, bulbs, pith, bark, and fruits. Since fruit is scarce in the Virungas, mountain gorillas tend to eat more foods growing on the ground, where their western lowland relatives eat fruit more often, rivaling the chimpanzee as top fruit eater.

Western lowland gorillas feed on 239 known types of food, including the fruits from 77 plant species. They prefer fleshy fruits when they can get them, but will switch to more fibrous fruits and herbaceous plants, such as arrowroots and aromatic plants, such as Afromomum, when fruit is scarce in the dry season. Even when fruits are in season, they will eat aquatic herbs and the fibrous parts of plants with a high protein and mineral content. In the Likoula region of north-central Congo, western lowland gorillas spend part of their year exclusively in the swamp forests, where they feed on the aquatic plants.

Eastern lowland gorillas change their diet with the seasons. The 48 species of fruit they consume make up no more than a quarter of food items.

TRACKING GORILLAS

The key to studying gorillas is the process of "habituation," when gorillas are followed for months by researchers until they accept the presence of people and then ignore them. The first groups to become habituated were mountain gorillas, and much of what we know about the behavior of gorillas in the wild is from the studies of these animals. Lowland gorillas, particularly those in Gabon and Cameroon, are more flighty than mountain gorillas, because they have been hunted so heavily and are wary of people. The number of studies has increased during the past 15 years, and gorillas in the northern region of the Republic of Congo, for example, are allowing field researchers to approach more closely. Nevertheless, scientists have had to rely on studies such as the analysis of dung in night nests simply to find out what they eat. They can estimate population sizes by counting nests.

1. (opposite) A mountain gorilla feeds on bamboo shoots found on the slopes of its mountain home.

During the dry season, when fruit becomes scarce, they turn to leaves and bark, as well as herbaceous plants similar to those eaten by western lowland gorillas. They appear to have a dietary regime that is halfway between the mainly leaf-eating diet, or folivory, of mountain gorillas and fruit-eating diet, frugivory, of western lowland gorillas.

Where trees are strong enough to support their weight, mountain gorillas will climb up to 30 m into the forest canopy in order to reach their favorite fruits and flowers, such as the plum-sized fruits produced by oak-like Pygeum trees growing on mountain ridges, or the blossoms of Vernonia trees on the lower slopes. Bracket fungi on tree trunks are also sought after. Subordinate members of a group will try to hide the fungus, carrying it many yards from the tree so that it is not stolen. If there is a dispute, the silverback wades in and takes the fungus for himself. However, the smaller and less dominant members of the group can find more when foraging at altitudes of 9800 ft (3000 m). Here, a favorite food plant, *Loranthus luteo-aurantiacus,* a relative of mistletoe, is found solely on spindly trees such as *Hypericum lanceolatus* (related to St. John's wort) that are accessible only to smaller gorillas. The bulky adults resort to sitting under-neath and waiting for tidbits of leafy flowers to fall from above.

Animal protein

Gorillas rarely drink water since they obtain sufficient liquid in their food. They are not totally vegetarian because they often eat caterpillars, slugs, and snails accidentally with their salad. It is

3

1

2

COMMON FOODS AT DIFFERENT ALTITUDES

Alpine zone 11,500 ft (3500 m) and above
Mountain gorillas Lobelia and *Senecio*

Bamboo forest 8,000-9,800 ft (2500–3000 m)
Mountain gorillas bamboo (*Arundaria alpina*)

Mountain rain forest 4,900-11,500 ft (1500–3500 m)
Mountain gorillas 6,900-11,500 ft (2100–3500 m) Galium vine,
celery (*Peucedanum lineri*), nettles (*Laportea alatipes*), and thistles
(*Carduus afromontanus*)

Lowland - mountain rain forest 2,500-7,400 ft (760–2255 m)
Eastern lowland gorillas Fruit and *Aframomum* species

Lowland rain forest up to 5,000ft (1500 m)
Western lowland gorillas fruits, eg. persimmom fruits of *Diospyros*,
fruits of *Cola lizae*, and *Ganophyllum giganteum*, aquatic herbs

1. A female mountain gorilla feeds on thistles.

2. Vines, nettles, and celery are also favorite foods.

3. This female does not compete with other group members for food since she is surrounded by it.

⭐ Gorillas eat the mature fruits of the persimmon tree *Diospyros manii*, but avoid immature ones, which are covered with irritating hairs.

estimated that they eat several thousand invertebrates every day in this way, but most are tiny and amount to no more than about 2 g a day. They will deliberately pick out grubs and other juicy insect larvae to eat.

Mountain gorillas and eastern lowland gorillas also have a fondness for ants, especially six species of ants from the *Ponerinae* family that have a painful sting. They search for ant nests, including the nests of nomadic driver ants, and if they find one, they scoop up a handful, and lick them up, often slapping their arms and legs as the aggressive ants bite or sting through their fur. Western lowland gorillas eat weaver ants, but they also like termites. Instead of fishing for them by using a piece of grass like chimpanzees, they use sheer brute strength to break into the termite mounds, grabbing handfuls of inmates and stuffing them into their mouths. Ants and termites provide gorillas with more animal protein than they would get from eating other insects during the same bout of feeding, but ant and termite meals are rare and not thought to be of great nutritional importance. They are more of a special treat. Immature gorillas tend to eat more ants than adult females do, and silverbacks have not been seen to eat them at all.

A balanced diet

Studies of gorilla dung have shown that they try to follow a balanced diet. They choose certain succulent fruits for their sugar content, for instance, and the seeds of some fruits that have a low fat content. In general, gorillas tend to avoid fatty fruits.

1

Plant stems and bark provide fiber, and new leaves are rich in protein. They steer clear of vegetation laced with defensive plant poisons, like those with high levels of alkaloids—caffeine, morphine, and strychnine—although they are not so sensitive to phenols and tannins which are bitter substances that make plant materials unpalatable to animals.

Gorillas eat enormous quantities of food in order to sustain their bulk. A large male mountain gorilla might consume 50 lb (23 kg) of vegetation in a day. They cause some damage to foliage by trampling it, yet they do not strip a feeding site bare. Cattle and buffalo, with their sharp hooves, tend to slice into plant stems, but the padded hands and feet of the gorillas push plants into the soil without damage. Shoots sprout from the semi-buried stems, and plants such as nettle and thistles grow rapidly.

They are selective feeders so there is always sufficient vegetation left behind for regrowth. However, it is thought to be unlikely that they actually "manage" their habitat as the home ranges of several gorilla groups overlap. There would be no point in deliberately leaving plants untouched, since another group might come along and pull them up. Fortunately, their mountain forests are filled with a great diversity of edible plants and even several groups of hungry gorillas passing through the same area will fail to strip it bare.

1. Lowland gorillas mainly eat fruit, although when it is scarce they turn to foliage and stems.

 EATING DIRT

In the dry season, mountain gorillas sometimes dig into exposed areas of weathered subsoil and eat it. The soil consists of volcanic rocks and minerals, such as quartz, apatite, and magnetite. The soil is rich in calcium and potassium and it also contains iron, aluminium, sodium, and bromide salts, which may cure intestinal ailments. It also has clay, which the animals eat to neutralize plant poisons in their food. The gorilla scoops out the soil, then pulverizes it in its hand, grinding the coarse sandy material into fine particles. On Mount Visoke in Rwanda's Virunga mountains, mountain gorillas have excavated such large holes beneath tree roots that they have dug their own extensive "caves."

Mountain gorillas supplement their diet with rock minerals.

SOCIAL LIFE

SOCIAL LIFE

Gorillas live in the most stable social groups of all the great apes. The biggest threat to the family comes from another gorilla, particularly a lone silverback, or leading male, without his own group, and the resident silverback must be strong enough to fight off any rival. Adult gorillas may remain together for many years, and their groups vary in size. Mountain gorillas tend to live in larger family groups than lowland gorillas and are mainly leaf eaters. By living in a great salad bowl filled with edible plants, they face little competition between group members for food. They can afford to have large families, and forage over relatively small areas, covering about half a mile a day. Lowland gorillas, on the other hand, are fruit eaters and, because fruits are seasonal and limited in quantity, there is often competition for the best fruit trees. Lowland groups in West Africa have fewer members and travel greater distances, up to 2 miles a day.

Previous page: A mountain gorilla group interacts during its midday rest period. Mother and babies play together, but there is little mutual grooming as seen in other primates.

LIFE IN THE HAREM

Mountain and lowland gorillas both typically live in relatively small family groups headed by the largest and strongest male, the silverback. There is usually an immature male between 8 and 13 years old present, and a harem of three or four adult females and their respective offspring, usually 3 to 6 youngsters under eight years old. Groups may consist of 2 to 35 individuals, and there are also solitary individuals, as well as multi-male, all-female, and bachelor groups. The mixed group of 5 to 10 is the most common.

Although some females may remain with a silverback throughout their lives, the composition of a group does not remain the same forever. Youngsters grow up and emigrate, and changing circumstances, such as the death of a silverback or a chance encounter with a group led by a more "charismatic" male, can result in adult females and immature males leaving, too. When young females mature they are often enticed to another troop, where either they join another silverback's harem or they leave to start up a new troop with a lone male. In other primate groups, such as in troops of baboons, females tend to stay and are therefore related to each other. Mature female gorillas in a group, on the other hand, are unrelated. This arrangement brings with it all types of problems. As unrelated females, the chances are that they will come into conflict, particularly at feeding sites or in competitions for access to the silverback, and there are few social mechanisms to reduce tension. There is a type of pecking order, which can be seen when

1. Gorillas communicate vocally, but an enormous amount is said in a simple facial expression.

2. The large, dominant silverback is the focus for a group of mountain gorillas during a rest period.

1. A female mountain gorilla grooms the silverback, but he would be unlikely to groom a female in the group.

gorillas move off in single file, because the more dominant individuals are in the front, but this flimsy hierarchy fails to resolve serious conflicts as it might in other primate groups.

Keeping the peace

Adult gorillas rarely groom each other. Mothers and babies will groom, and so will related females. Females will groom the silverback, but he is unlikely to groom a female in return. Chimpanzees and baboons groom to calm things down and reinforce the bonds between individuals, as well as to keep their fur free of parasites and dirt. For

gorillas, one way to diffuse a situation is to involve a third party, for example another gorilla can be sought for protection or reassurance. This is a strategy adopted by immature females and subordinate males, but not by mature females. Young gorillas might also seek help or assurance from their mothers, and females will solicit protection from adult males.

Mother gorillas tend to stick together, and related females still living in the group into which they were born will support one another. Unrelated females rarely do, although long-term residents might form alliances. They may assist a fellow long-term resident and will be helped in return, but this aid is not extended to a new immigrant. New immigrants are greeted with a wall of aggression. This can be recognized because a group's traveling and eating times increase, rest periods decrease, and mothers and their offspring spend more time together. It is a tense time. If females join a group that is already large, they are more likely to be harassed by the resident females because the silverback's ability to intervene and subdue the conflict is diluted.

In reality, it is the silverback who maintains social harmony. As his level of aggression rises, aggression between females diminishes. Same-sex opponents tend to avoid each other, but if this is not possible, they inevitably fight, either verbally or physically. If a screaming fight occurs, the silverback will race in and cuff the two protagonists. If coalitions are formed between more than two animals and they all gang up on a single gorilla, the silverback intervenes and the alliance is dissolved. When things have settled down, the females involved in the disturbance might appease the silverback, although they are unlikely to be reconciled with each other.

As a whole, female gorillas have little time for each other, and the benefits of a relationship with the silverback far outweigh any among the group's females. As a consequence, females interact more with the dominant male than they do with each other. In fact, female gorillas stop feeding when the silverback walks into view and focus their attention on him. They only pay attention to females with whom they have a hostile relationship.

 GORILLA DISEASES AND PARASITES

Wild gorillas suffer a range of viral and bacterial illnesses, and support internal parasites. Mountain gorillas show symptoms that resemble the common cold, for instance. Many gorillas are also infested with nematode worms similar to the human hookworm. Some have been found with roundworm larvae in the blood, and tapeworms and roundworms in the intestines. Western lowland gorillas have been found with the tick *Rhipicicephalus appendiculatus*, which carries tickbite fever in humans. Some have been seen to suffer from a condition not unlike yaws, a contagious disease that can cause severe scarring and deformity. Others show a bacterial skin infection similar to leprosy. Lowland gorillas also have flukes, and have been found with several species of disease-causing organisms, such as those causing malaria.

FAMILY TALK

The silverback is the undisputed leader of the troop. Aggressive stares and head jerks from him are usually enough to keep the peace. In fact, gorillas have many facial expressions that convey their state of mind to others in the troop. They have a wide-eyed play face and a lip tuck to indicate tension, yawning reveals stress, and a protruding tongue conveys uncertainty or concentration. When a silverback is frightened or angry the hairs on his head crest stand erect.

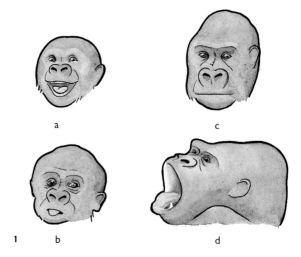

One strange behavior that is shown by western lowland gorillas is hand clapping by females and juveniles. They seem to do this when they are nervous, and the sound alerts the silverback to potential danger, such as an approaching field researcher. The silverback responds with a single roar. Communication is not only by body language or hand clapping, but also with a repertoire of hoots, grunts, coughs, burps, belches, snorts, and hiccups. There are about 15 distinct vocalizations recognized from mountain gorillas. A territorial hoot call, which travels a couple of miles through the forest, is similar to that produced by chimpanzees, suggesting that their common ancestor would have made a similar sound.

Gorillas often do not make eye contact when foraging, so a series of grunts keeps the troop in touch with each other. Pig-like grunts and snorts seem to establish an individual's right of way when foraging. Deep belch vocalizations or double grunts are often heard when feeding, resting, moving, or when engaged in social activities, which suggests

1. Facial expressions: (a) a baby gorilla smiling after being tickled; (b) a young gorilla showing his tongue when concentrating; (c) an adult male's lip sucking or tight-lipped face; (d) an adult male yawning.

2. A penetrating stare from the silverback is enough to put an unruly group member in its place.

3. Even a silverback must sleep. His nest is usually on the ground while others build nests in trees and bushes.

3

NEST BUILDERS

Gorillas construct a fresh nest each night by bending plants together to make a strong platform about 80–100 cm in diameter. Adult males remain on or close to the ground. The larger the gorilla the closer to the ground it sleeps. A ground nest can consist of grasses, twigs, or foliage, although in bamboo thickets, gorillas have been seen to bend and weave a night nest of bamboo stems into a natural "spring mattress." Juveniles and females with babies tend to build their night nests in the forks of trees. The same method is adopted by most gorillas. First, the animal pulls three stout branches toward itself, bending them over and pressing them together with its feet. Smaller branches are woven into the structure and the bottom is lined with a cushion of twigs and leaves.

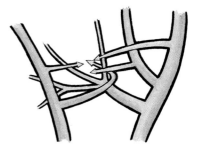

Smaller branches are woven together to create the nest's platform-like structure.

that they mean "all's well" and that the animal is content. There appear to be two types, a double grunt with a low second part, which is given after a period of silence and which elicits a reply, and a double grunt with a higher second part, which is given by an animal within five seconds of another grunting. The call is complex, since each double grunt is specific to an individual animal, and high-ranking animals tend to grunt more. Researchers in the field are taught to learn and mimic these sounds when following a troop of gorillas.

Gorillas also "purr" on sunny days, occasionally make a "humm" sound, give a bo-bo-bo call when spread out in the forest, and "neigh" like a horse when interested in the opposite sex. Youngsters "chuckle" when playing and young blackback males bark if they spot potential danger approaching or want to threaten another gorilla. Screams and roars are emitted in traumatic situations, when females are fighting, or when a group is confronted by people. The loudest, most intense roars are delivered by angry silverbacks and blackbacks.

Protection racket

Each of the animals in a troop may beat their chests at some point in the day. It is a way of saying "I'm excited" or "I'm nervous." However, the full charging display is the province of the leading male, and it follows a set ritual of vocalizations and demonstrative body language in nine recognizable steps. To begin with, the silverback hoots, slowly at first and then faster. He pretends to feed, but as the intensity of the display increases, he stands upright

☆ Gorillas spend about 45 percent of their waking hours feeding, 33 percent resting, and 22 percent traveling.

1. A silverback mountain gorilla performs his threat display. He is telling the photographer to back off.

2. The silverback mountain gorilla named Ziz is beating his chest as part of the threat display.

3. The first two stages of the silverback's threat display are hooting slowly and then faster (a). The succeeding stages are pretending to feed (b), throwing vegetation (c), beating his chest (d), a one-leg kick (e), running (f), tearing at vegetation (g), and thumping the ground.

a

b

c

2

1. (opposite) An open mouth, revealing the large canine teeth, is part of this silverback lowland gorilla's threat display.

2. A yawn from a silverback mountain gorilla exposes formidable jaws and teeth, a reminder of the damage they might do.

Field researchers can recognize individual gorillas by face and body shape, and also by nose shape. Each "nose-print" is different, like human fingerprints.

and begins to throw vegetation. The fifth stage is to beat his chest with cupped hands, followed by a one-leg kick. Then he runs bipedally and on all fours while he slaps and tears at the vegetation. The display ends with him thumping the ground with the palms of his hands.

Gorillas are mainly passive and shy animals, and silverbacks only put on these displays to scare off an intruder or to give the rest of the troop a chance to flee into the forest. A display might be used to warn off a lone silverback looking for females or hoping to take over a troop. The challenge can become intense, but it rarely develops into a full-blown fight. If two groups should meet, for example, an exchange of hooting might end with the leading silverbacks from each group sizing each other up. The larger, older, and more confident individual might strut up to the other and stop no more than 3 to 6 feet away. The two assume rigid stances but both avert their gaze. The rest of the opposing troops sit motionless, waiting to see what will happen. One of the males, often the younger of the two, will break the silence and begin his chest-beating display. The older male might then be triggered into action. Dispensing with the display he might simply roar and charge, the young silverback fleeing rapidly.

If a fight follows all the troop is at risk of injury, especially youngsters who can get trampled and badly injured, or even killed. It benefits all the members in a group, therefore, to have the most powerful silverback leading and protecting them. For this reason, the silverback is a female gorilla's most important ally.

A DAY IN THE LIFE …

Gorillas, like the other great apes, wander around a defined home range where all their food is found, and stop at traditional resting sites within it. Mountain gorillas rise between six and eight o'clock in the morning. If it is raining, and it rains at some time every day in the forest, they may "lie in" and wait for it to stop. They then eat a substantial sit-down "brunch" until about midday. The adults rest and digest their food, while the youngsters play. The forest is like a natural playground, where young gorillas can hone their forest skills and learn how to interact with other gorillas. They often climb into the trees to play. At around two o'clock in the afternoon, the large male rises and the entire group is galvanized into action. He leads his family away into the forest, where they travel slowly for anywhere between 330-6,600 ft (100–2000 m), snacking as they go. They defecate while walking, without changing posture or pace, and leave a considerable quantity of dung behind, about 20 to 35 three-lobed pieces from each gorilla per day. The dung has a similar texture and smell to horse dung.

At about five or six o'clock in the early evening, the large male stops and the entire group begins constructing its night nests. At about six o'clock, they turn in and sleep until about six the following morning. At least, this is what we think they do, since there have been few studies of mountain gorillas at night. It is known, however, that they defecate in and around their nests once or twice during the night and once before rising. Because

 LIVING TOGETHER

Lowland gorillas are not always alone. They sometimes share their patch of forest with their close relatives, the chimpanzees. They seem to make amicable neighbors and do not appear to fight over food, even though they rely on the same fruits. Each species tends to adjust its group size in response to the availability of food, and split into smaller subgroups when food is scarce or widely spread. Chimpanzees will do this readily, but gorillas, with their more easily available high-fiber diet, have less need to split up and tend to remain in larger foraging parties. Both species construct their night nests in trees, although chimpanzees tend to nest in primary forest, sites that have always been forested, while lowland gorillas nest in secondary forest, which has grown in once unforested areas.

1. A female mountain gorilla rests at midday.

2. A silverback mountain gorilla relaxes during a daytime rest period. These are often extended during rare sunny periods.

their diet produces so much gas, they also belch and pass wind fairly frequently. Some have been seen to suffer short bursts of hiccups.

Gorillas yawn in the same way as people do, often when they are uneasy. A modest yawn involves raising the head and opening the mouth, but during a high intensity yawn, the head tips back and the mouth opens wide, exposing the teeth and black, cavernous mouth.

While resting, mountain gorillas will sit or lie on one side while they groom themselves. Shoulders and arms are groomed using one hand alone. The hair is pushed against the grain and held in place by the mouth or chin, while the hand investigates for parasites, dirt, or dead skin. The abdomen, chest, and legs are groomed with both hands, one to hold back the hair and the other to pick at the skin. They also scratch vigorously, moving four fingers against the fur, sometimes along the entire length of the arm or abdomen. Similar to a person scratching their head, the gorilla scratches its arms if unsure of a situation. If it scratches something delicate, such as the corner of the eye, it uses the index finger. The index finger is also used to pick the nose and teeth.

1. Mountain gorillas seek out the shelter of trees and thick vegetation, and sit with folded arms when resting during heavy rain or hail storms.

2. Mountain gorillas foraging in a forest clearing in the Virunga Mountains.

2

Lowland gorillas

Only a small amount of research has been done on lowland gorillas, but the little work that has been achieved has revealed that they follow a similar schedule to their mountain relatives. They rise just after dawn, and begin to forage in their 6–36 sq. km home range, following a travel schedule that takes into account certain foods that come into season at the same time each year. They can be seen in a fruit tree above the ground, since they are good climbers, or in a swampy clearing, where they wade up to their armpits in water and feed on the roots and tubers of aquatic plants.

The group spreads out while feeding to reduce competition and conflict, but after a few hours it comes together again for the midday rest. The adults lie down and digest, snoozing or grooming while the youngsters play. In the afternoon, the gorillas either indulge in "travel feeding," during which they ▷▷

PRIMATE CLASSIFICATION: GORILLAS

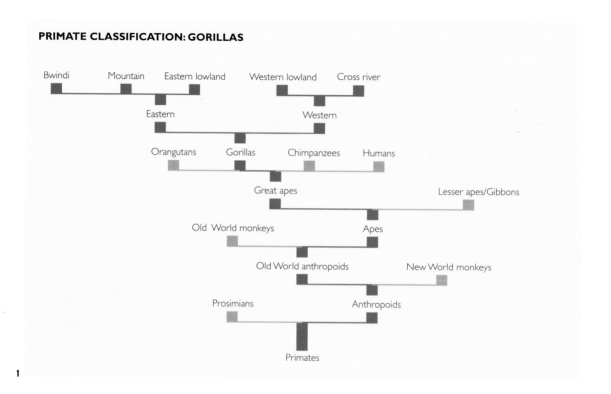

1

Previous page: A family group of western lowland gorillas socializes during a daytime rest period.

1. There are two species of gorilla: the eastern gorilla (*Gorilla berengei*) and the western gorilla (*Gorilla gorilla*), each of which is further divided into subspecies.

2. An eastern lowland gorilla, recognized by its uniformly black hair, dozes during the day.

 EVOLUTION

The great apes, including orangutans, gorillas, chimpanzees, and bonobos, are the largest living primates and humankind's closest relatives. They are descended from African monkeys. Ape-like fossils are found in rocks over 20 million years old. They first to split off from the evolutionary tree were the gibbons about 16 to 20 million years ago. The gorillas split away 6 to 8 million years ago. The human line diverged from the chimpanzees 4 to 5 million years ago.

move around and eat a little, or the silverback leads them directly to a fruiting tree where they can feast on their favorite fruits. If the silverback has a grown-up son in the group, the silverback leads the way, the rest traveling behind him single file, and the son brings up the rear. In a group without any other adult males, an older female leads and the silverback is the rear guard. In the evening they pitch camp and, like the mountain gorillas, build nests in which they spend the night.

One group of western lowland gorillas studied at Bai Hokoeu in the Dzanga-Ndoki National Park, in the Central African Republic was found to be led by two silverbacks rather than one. The group ranged over a wide area of about 8.8 sq mi (22.9 sq km), covering 1.43mi (2.3 km) a day on average. It differed from other groups because it splits into two distinct subgroups when foraging, and, on some occasions, the two slept 2 miles apart.

The distance covered by gorilla groups during the day varies between species and depends on what they are eating. The Bai Hokoeu gorillas, for example, travel an average of 1.9mi (3.1 km) per day when eating mainly fruit, but manage only 1.3mi (2.1 km)

2

1

when fruit is scarce and they switch to other vegetation, such as leaves, bark, and pithy stems. The distance traveled increases noticeably when patches of fruit are small. Of all the gorilla populations, the Bai Hokoeu groups forage over the greatest distances, with an average daily journey throughout the year of 1.6mi (2.6 km). This compares with an average of 1.07mi (1.7 km) a day for lowland gorillas in Gabon and just .3mi (0.5 km) for mountain gorillas in the Virunga mountains.

Foraging gorillas, particularly lowland gorillas, are often not alone, because following them are African jacanas. These birds take advantage of the insects flushed out by the gorillas, and are more successful when feeding alongside gorillas than when alone.

The trees also profit from gorilla activity, because the groups distribute their seeds as they travel and forage. The gorillas eat the fruits, the seeds are passed through the gut, and then they are dispersed through their dung. This ensures that they germinate some distance away from the parent plant. Some plants seem to depend exclusively on gorillas for seed dispersal. In the Lope Reserve in Gabon, for example, the fruits of the tree *Cola lizae* are a primary food source for lowland gorillas. While other primates eat the flesh only, the gorillas swallow large seeds, and an estimated 11,000 to 18,000 seeds are distributed by gorillas in every square mile of forest during the four-month fruiting season.

Seeds deposited in gorilla dung germinate better than those sprouting elsewhere. The best survival rate is 40 percent and is found at the gorillas' nests which are in the more open areas of the forest where there is more light and less competition from other plants.

2

1. It rains incessantly in the Virunga Mountains, and mountain gorillas show cold-like symptoms.

2. A western lowland gorilla feeds on fruit, the animal's primary food.

There are only about 600 mountain gorillas surviving in Rwanda, Congo, and Uganda. They live in an area that has been racked by wars.

BLACKBACKS AND SILVERBACKS

BLACKBACKS AND SILVERBACKS

Silver-gray hair gives a distinguished look to a human male, and the same colored hair on a gorilla turns him into an impressive and powerful leader. As a male gorilla matures, he acquires a magnificent saddle of silver hair on his back and is known as a silverback. A young male does not have this badge of status, and is known as a blackback. Blackbacks, however, often have an interest in females in their group, and the females tolerate this attention. Some females even groom young blackback males, an insurance policy, perhaps, for the future. Juveniles sometimes associate with blackbacks and may follow them around.

Some blackbacks desert their groups before they reach maturity. They travel alone until accepted by another group, or wait until they reach silverback status and fight to take over a group. The transition from blackback to silverback is just one part of growing up in the wild.

Previous page:
A young mountain gorilla rides on its mother's back, and will until it can keep up with the group by itself.

GROWING UP

A baby gorilla is born 250 to 285 days after conception, compared to an average of 226 days in the chimpanzee. The birth often happens at night in the mother's night nest, although births also occur in the afternoon. Labor lasts about 30 minutes, during which the baby is born head first in the same way as a human baby. The baby's head is much smaller than that of a newborn human, however, making it easier to pass down the birth canal. A baby gorilla weighs just 3-5 LB (1.4–2.3 kg) at birth. Gorillas, like chimpanzees and orangutans, usually give birth to a single baby. They rarely have twins and if they do,

one inevitably dies, because the mother cannot care for two. Difficult births can take longer than half-an-hour and, strangely, the rest of the group can behave aggressively toward the mother during labor.

The gorilla baby is small and helpless at first, with only a little fur on its pinkish-gray skin. Its limb movements are uncoordinated, it cannot focus its gaze, and it is startled by loud noises. The birth fluids are licked away immediately after birth, and the mother usually eats the placenta, because in the wild, nothing nutritious goes to waste. The baby is clutched belly to belly and groomed by its mother within 45 minutes of birth. Gorilla mothers, ▷▷

1. A baby mountain gorilla, just two hours old, is totally dependent on its mother. She holds it close in case inquisitive youngsters in the group hurt it.

1

1. A lowland gorilla youngster, like its mountain relatives, rides on its mother's back. It may travel in this way for months.

1

like human mothers, tend to cradle their offspring on their left side, especially male infants. This differs from orangutans and gibbons, which do not show any carrying preference. As the baby's muscles strengthen, it shows a rhythmic "rooting" movement of its head when searching for its mother's breast and it will call softly to encourage its mother to help it in the correct suckling position. Like a human baby, it has a strong grasp, but differs because it has strong back and neck muscles much earlier than a human baby.

At 2 to 5 weeks old the gorilla infant smiles and makes noises that sound almost as if it is laughing. Its gaze is coordinated by about six weeks, and its reaching movements are coordinated by seven weeks. Hand-eye coordination is achieved by 9 to 10 weeks. It can crawl at about nine weeks, but still travels around by grasping the long chest hairs on its mother's underside, occasionally supported by her hand when moving fast. It takes its first solid food by about 10 to 12 weeks old. At 16 weeks, the mother lifts her baby onto her back, where it rides clinging on to its mother's fur with both hands and feet, and some infants have even been seen to grasp an arm or leg while the mother ambles along.

The baby can walk and climb by itself at six months old, by which time it has learned how to beat its chest. It still relies mainly on its mother's milk, but is able to pluck at and eat vegetation, albeit without the ability to prepare it, like stripping off leaves from the stem. Most solid food items are supplied, however, by its mother. The young gorilla may attempt to build its first nest at eight months, although it will remain in its mother's night nest for a further two to three years, or until she gives birth again. At first, youngsters build flimsy nests of leaves, patting down stalks or rearranging foliage during day resting periods, but practice makes perfect and eventually they are able to construct a solid, well-formed nest. The youngest mountain gorilla to build and sleep in its own night nest during the late Dian Fossey's study in the Virungas was 34 months old. By the end of its first year, the young gorilla will stray from its mother for short periods of time to investigate the other members of the troop. During its early years, it may make whining, crying, or chuckling sounds.

Gorilla babies receive a lot of care during the three years before weaning, however, almost half of all baby gorillas fail to make it to their third birthday. They die mainly in their first year from infant diseases, predation, and injuries sustained as a result of rival silverbacks fighting. On rare occasions, an infant can be the victim of cannibalism. Dian Fossey recalled a time in 1976 when a mountain gorilla mother was holding a six-month old baby ventrally, or to her front, rather than carrying it on her back. The mother had been harassed previously by a subordinate male and his allies. One day, the baby simply disappeared. An

1

intensive search over the terrain covered by the mother's group revealed nothing, and there were no signs of an incursion by another group. Suspecting the worst and "chilled at the implications of cannibalism," Fossey decided to collect and analyze dung samples. They found minute slivers of bone and infant hair in the dung of the gorillas who had victimized the mother.

Rough and tumble

The young mountain gorillas who survive these disturbing events indulge in play. They play games such as tag, king of the castle, tug of war with stalks of vegetation, and even "catch" with grape-fruit-sized fruits known locally as mtanga tanga. The gorillas do not eat this particular fruit, yet the youngsters climb high into the trees to knock it down. They throw it into the air and even perform fair imitations of baseball, football, and soccer. They also hang around and swing in the trees, but do so far less than young chimpanzees. Play fights and touching games usually take place between two individuals, while chasing games may be played with three. There is a sexual difference, however. Young males will play with females and other males, but young females seldom play together. The silverback seems to be tolerant of them all as they clamber over him.

In captivity, lowland silverbacks in small social groups have been seen to play short rough-and-tumble games with infants, whereas play with older females is slower, more relaxed, and lasts longer. It is thought that the adult male is compensating for a lack of peers with which the youngster would ▷▷

2

1. A mountain gorilla shows an interest in his newborn sister. Gorillas are often curious about new additions to the group.

2. Baby gorillas are vulnerable and only about half of them survive until their third birthday.

⭐ A female gorilla produces a surviving offspring only once every six to eight years during her breeding life.

1

 INFANTS IN DANGER

About 38 percent of baby gorillas are killed not by disease or predators, but by attacks from unrelated male gorillas. The threat of infanticide is one of the driving forces that encourages gorillas to group together. Both females and baby gorillas need to be protected by a large and powerful male in order to survive. If a silverback should die or is otherwise missing, any youngsters that are not close to being weaned are likely to be killed by an unfamiliar male. By killing the progeny of the previous male, he will stimulate the females in the group to become fertile and be ready to bear his offspring instead. Death is usually caused by a bite to the head and groin. Groups with more than one male, maybe with a dominant silverback, older blackback, and "retired" silverback, are more successful at meeting challenges from other males.

1. This three-week-old baby is its 27-year-old mother's sixth offspring. It can expect expert care from such an experienced parent.

2. (opposite) A lowland gorilla mother clutches her baby. Many inexperienced mothers in captivity abandon their babies, and they have to be reared by their human keepers.

normally play. In the wild, adults sometimes join games. Dian Fossey describes how one of the mountain gorilla groups she studied was coming down from the alpine zone above 4000 m through several rows of tall Senecio trees. Led by a mature male, the entire group loped from one tree to the next in a kind of square dance routine, twirling around each bough before reaching out for the next. When they came to the end, they climbed back up the slope and did it all over again . . . and again. Play behavior is important for an animal with a long childhood. During these sessions it must learn how to survive in an often hostile environment. They are times when a young gorilla can exercise its growing limbs and muscles, discover which foods are good to eat and where they are found, learn how to fight, and appreciate social etiquette. Another reason to play is to relieve boredom.

1

Like human teenagers, juveniles wanting some action but constrained by a "resting" session will play games, such as catching flies between the palms of the hands, pulling them apart, and going cross eyed as every tiny piece is carefully examined. Occasionally, when without play partners, they will clap their hands or the soles of their feet and slap the underside of their jaw so that it makes a rhythmic clackety-clack sound, during which other youngsters

1. A nine-year-old lowland gorilla plays a boisterous game with a two-year-old youngster.

2. Young males often play with gorillas younger than themselves, but subadult females rarely do so.

2

1. Young gorillas often play in the trees, but as they grow older they tend to climb less and spend more time on the ground.

2. This young mountain gorilla survived being caught in a poacher's snare, but it lost a hand. Nevertheless, it can climb effectively in the trees.

3. (opposite) Silverbacks are tolerant of youngsters at play. This young silverback mountain gorilla allows a juvenile to play bite his belly.

may pirouette. They will also stalk animals, following harmless creatures that range in size from frogs to the small deer of the forest known as duikers. The young gorillas are clearly intent on capturing them. Two of the youngsters being studied in the Virungas happened upon a baby duiker hiding in the undergrowth and were seen to capture and play with it. One gorilla pulled at its legs and lifted its head while the other stared at and stroked the fawn's trembling body.

Developing skills about twice as fast as a human baby, an infant gorilla is fully weaned at 2 to 2½ years old. During this first couple of years, its mother will gradually reduce the amount of contact until it eventually becomes independent.

Males mature at about 12 years old, but rarely breed successfully until they are about 15 years old. Females reach sexual maturity at about 8 years old, but do not begin to breed until they are about 10 years old.

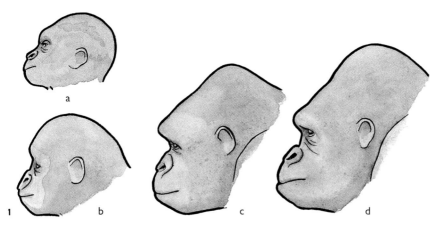

1. Changes in the shape of gorillas' heads: from baby male (a) to adult male (d); and from baby female (b) to adult female (c).

2. A dominant silverback mountain gorilla sits with his son. In this group, the son eventually took over from his father.

a

b

c

d

1

2

TAKING OVER THE FAMILY BUSINESS

During a gorilla's lifetime, the greatest changes are seen on the male's body. While all gorillas have gray hair when they are older, silverbacks have a silver-gray saddle across their backs and upper thighs. Blackbacks may become silverbacks at 10 to 12 years old, and the accompanying hormonal changes trigger secondary sexual characteristics. The bony crests on the male's head grow taller, and the hair on his arms grows longer, while that on his chest is lost. A hairless chest produces a more resonant sound when the male performs his chest-beating display. Gorillas have no hair on their fingers, the palms of their hands, the soles of their feet and their armpits. In all, the mature silverback will have grown into a conspicuously powerful animal.

When mature, some males leave the group and travel alone until they find an area where they can settle down and attract their own females. Some are driven out by their dominant silverback fathers. Usually, however they leave of their own accord. These are young males that have reached maturity while their father is still young. With little chance of inheriting the crown, and rather than waste their reproductive life, they leave. Some young males join with others to form bachelor groups. They roam the countryside, approaching mixed bands in the hope of enticing females to join them. The males in these mixed bands, despite being unrelated, tend to stay closer together and interact more than males in single-sex groups. They are also more aggressive than males in single-sex groups, but for some reason they often stare at each other. Young and subordinate animals gaze at older, dominant ones

 SEX DIFFERENCES

Male and female gorillas are substantially different, males are significantly larger than the females. Females are about 1 ft (30 cm) shorter and about half the weight of males. On average, males are 5.5 ft (1.7 m) tall and weigh 395 lb (180 kg), while females are under 5 ft (1.5 m) and 200 lb (90 kg). Males in captivity tend to be substantially more obese than their wild cousins. The heaviest specimen was Ngagi, a male mountain gorilla held in the San Diego Zoo, in the 1940s. Although no more than 5.5 ft (1.72 m) tall, at his heaviest he weighed a staggering 680 lb (310 kg). Male mountain gorillas are much bigger than male lowland gorillas, while the females of both subspecies are similar in size. Females have an earlier spurt of growth than males, although males eventually grow much bigger. On the head, the male gorilla's crests are taller than the female's and his chest is hairless.

1. (opposite) This silverback (left) joined his group as an immature stranger, but when he grew up he took over as leader after turmoil caused by poachers.

2. Juvenile mountain gorillas indulge in a bout of play fighting. Neither will harm the other, but it could be a rehearsal for real and bloody fights later in life.

2

probably for greeting or appeasement. It also triggers play and sexual interactions. If females join the group, however, these males become intolerant of each other.

A male can also live a solitary life. His daily pattern is similar to that of a male in a group, except that he travels farther and ranges wider. He makes contact with many different groups, and on his travels he gathers information about the location of these groups. As he matures, he gathers useful knowledge about the health and status of the groups' silverbacks, so he is ready to take over if one should die or be deposed. Once he has gained females, his home range shrinks.

Some blackbacks remain at home, but whether they take over their father's group depends on his age when they reach maturity. If a male is born when his father is old, he will be too young when the time comes to take over, so it is only males that

are born around the middle of their father's life that have the opportunity to take over the group successfully. The transfer of power is usually gradual, although healed bite wounds on the body of the heir apparent indicate that while he was growing up, life in the family was not always peaceful. Apart from being put in his place by the silverback, interactions between father and son will have been few. They would have avoided each other to reduce the like-lihood of aggressive encounters. When the heir takes over, the old silverback is allowed to remain in his group and live out the rest of his days in relative peace.

Asserting dominance

Such is a dominant silverback's power that just a look from him is enough to quell disorder in the group. He will sometimes use force to grab ▷▷

1. Playtime for juvenile mountain gorillas is usually the midday rest period.

2. This young blackback mountain gorilla was photographed while play fighting. The open mouth and showing of teeth indicate that the intensity of the combat is getting close to the real thing.

1

▷ TAKING RISKS

Leaving the safety of the dominant silverback and going out alone is risky, and males are more likely to be killed than females. The number of head injuries in lowland gorillas suggests that there is considerable risk of being attacked by another gorilla. Gorillas show twice as many head injuries as chimpanzees and bonobos. Leopards are a danger, too. Despite their size, gorillas are outmanouvered occasionally by leopards. In February 1961 there was an incident in Kigezi, Uganda, when a large silverback and a female gorilla were found dead within three days of each other. The male had been rushed in his night nest and had clearly put up a desperate fight, rolling down the slopes of Mt. Muhavura with his attacker. When his body was discovered, the neck was badly injured and a gash in its lower belly revealed where the leopard had started to eat the soft tissues. The female had also been partly eaten.

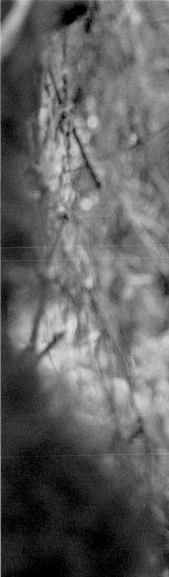

2

and hold down an unruly blackback. He will cuff any females that disturb his peace during a screaming fight. His aggression moderates the aggression in his females.

In an experiment in captivity, a dominant male was removed from a group of lowland gorillas. The level of aggression between females soared, and the interactions between mothers and their offspring increased. As soon as the male was returned, aggression levels gradually declined.

The silverback is like a benevolent dictator. He is concerned with the welfare of his entire group, but no member of the group is allowed to challenge his authority. He has the strength of six full-grown men, and he must be prepared to use it, because he will often be challenged by other males.

With a few males possessing most of the females, and many males with none, competition for the females is intense. During fighting, it is not only the male that is at risk. The biggest threat to a male's females and their offspring is that of another large, mature, male gorilla trying to take over his group. Fights can be severe, but if the male shows that he is bigger and stronger, bloodshed can be avoided. Being large has its advantages.

Competition between males, therefore, is the reason that male gorillas are so much larger than the females, an attribute known as sexual dimorphism. This trait is shared with other polygamous mammals, such as elephants, lions, elephant seals, and sea lions. Given the competition between males, and with the pressure of constant fighting, natural selection has favored the large and powerful male. As a result, gorillas have evolved into the most sexually dimorphic of all the primates. Males and females differ in size and appearance.

FEMALE CHOICE

Female gorillas leave the group in which they were born and go to other troops. They have a preference for lone males and males with small groups rather than large established groups. A large group may already have females that have formed alliances and a new female could have a hard time at first. Females do not necessarily remain with the first troop they join, and there are several factors that will determine whether they stay or move on. The quality of food in a group's home range could influence the decision, but more important is a silverback's ability to fight. A powerful male is more likely to protect her and her offspring. In order to win the affections of a female, the silverback must put on a good chest-beating display. She watches carefully, looking for symmetry in the face and body and a glossy coat, two indications that the male is healthy.

COURTSHIP AND MATING

Gorillas live for a long time. The oldest known wild gorilla died at 35 years old and some gorillas have reached the age of 50 or more in captivity. During their lifetime, female gorillas give birth every $3\frac{1}{2}$ to $4\frac{1}{2}$ years. Births can take place at any time during the year since there is no fixed season. The menstrual cycle lasts for about three and a half weeks and ovulation occurs in mid-cycle for about 2 to 3 days, compared to 10 to 14 days in chimpanzees and 5 to 6 days in orangutans. Menarche, or the first menstrual flow, starts at 6 to 7 years old and is slight. Unlike female chimpanzees, estrus, or being receptive to mating, in young female gorillas is marked only by a slight swelling of the genitalia.

Males tend to recognize receptive females not only by smell, but also by the female's behavior. The mature silverback stimulates sexual activity by performing his chest-beating display, followed by a stiff-legged strutting run during which he may cuff the female. The female stands stiffly and has a distinctive facial expression. Her lips are pressed together and the corners of her mouth are drawn in. This tight-lipped face is generally associated with apprehension. She may then encourage the male to mate by special glances and touches, and will then crouch low and back up to the male, all the while looking back at him. The male usually enters from behind, although belly to belly cop- ulation has also been seen. All the while, both male and female "coo" like doves.

About 40 percent of mountain gorilla groups have more than one male. In these groups, the

1. A female mountain gorilla rests her head on the back of the group's silverback. Females often court the group's leader rather than be with other females.

1

dominant silverback mates much more often than subordinate males. In fact, up to 83 percent of matings are by dominant males, and they have almost exclusive rights to the mature and pregnant females. Never-theless, some females in a group will have sexual relations with more than one male. Sometimes males and females that have been brought up in the same group have a sexual relationship, and females that have been in residence for a while may mate with an old, non-breeding male, although recent immigrants would not. Mating takes place only when a female is at the receptive point in her menstrual cycle, indicating that, unlike the bonobos, who have sex at the drop of a hat, mating in gorillas serves a primarily reproductive function.

In multi-male mountain gorilla groups, about one third of matings by subordinate males are interrupted by harassment from other males, particularly by the dominant male, although the chastisement is usually minor and the aggressive behavior relatively mild. Often, the silverback seems to be unable or unwilling to intervene. This means that there is a favorable place within a multi-male group for a young male to gain mating opportunities.

2

A baby gorilla that was rescued after its mother had been killed by poachers was seen to shed "tears" and make sob-like sounds.

1. Here mountain gorillas are mating. Copulation can be brief, lasting only a few minutes.

2. A mountain gorilla silverback and leader of the Susa group in the Virunga Mountains.

A LOW-KEY INTELLIGENCE

A LOW-KEY INTELLIGENCE

Gorillas often appear languid and indifferent. Mountain gorillas are surrounded by readily available food, so do they need to think? Are they "programed" to get up in the morning, forage in the forest, and then go back to bed? One gorilla was once seen to build its night nest with a roof. Was this a singular event, or are all gorillas capable of breaking out of their apparently repetitive lifestyle?

Compared to their close relatives, the chimpanzees and bonobos, gorillas seem dull, but you would be wrong if you thought they were unintelligent. While not as inquisitive as chimpanzees, they show more tenacity. They have good memories and in captivity are more likely to perform tasks out of interest rather than to earn a reward. They have shown to be capable of learning words of artificial languages, such as sign languages for the deaf, and of solving complex reasoning problems.

THE UNDERRATED APE

The gorilla's brain is much smaller in relation to its body size than that of a human. Its large head and high cranial crest serve only as attachments for its powerful chewing muscles. The average brain capacity of a 350 lb (160 kg) gorilla is 500 cc (0.5 liters), although some gorillas have larger brains, with one excep-tional individual recorded as having a 750 (0.75-liter) brain. By comparison, a 132 lb (60 kg) human has a brain size of about 1,400 cc (1.4 liters), so the ratio of brain size to body weight for the two species is 1:43 for humans and 1:320 for gorillas.

Whatever the size of a gorilla's brain, the animal must learn about its environment and update its behavior accordingly. Information is gathered through the five senses, hearing, sight, smell, taste, and touch. Gorillas need good hearing, because in the dense forest sight is less reliable in locating other members of the group or spotting danger. They are alert to sounds that are strange or out of context. If someone approaching a feeding group should break a twig accidentally, the chances are that the gorillas will ignore it. If the same thing should happen near a resting group, however, they will leap up instantly and check out the cause of the sound. The only sound at which they will flee immediately is the human voice.

Gorillas also have good eyesight, because they must be able to spot movements in the under-growth and find and identify the right foods to eat.

1. Gorillas can manipulate objects precisely using their fingers, in this case for a grooming session.

1. A male mountain gorilla looks around the surrounding forest, assessing his next meal. He will eat a variety of forest foods, processing them in different ways.

As daytime plant eaters, they probably have good color vision. Genetic studies have revealed that gorillas have the same genes that code for visual pigments as humans, so it is thought that they have the same color vision we do. This would be important, for example, in recognizing when fruits are ripening. Their eyes focus closer than human eyes, and they appear near sighted when studying food or when grooming. They watch their fingers from a distance of about 6 in (15 cm) or less and hold objects close to their eyes.

Gorillas have an average sense of smell, and in captivity are often seen to bring objects to their nose as if to smell them. In the wild, they can pick up strong odors such as human sweat or the musk of a rival male.

Male gorillas have a pungent body odor, which has been described as "a combination of human sweat, manure, and charred wood," particularly when excited. They have glands in the armpits that produce this powerful "fear" odor when confronting predators or rivals. Females produce this smell slightly.

Both males and females have glands on the palms of their hands and soles of the feet, which leave olfactory messages along their trails in their home range. A female's odor, a specific smell produced in her urine and around her genital organs, enables a silverback to determine her reproductive status. Like us, a gorilla jumps when startled and its heart rate goes up, although it is much slower than, say, a chimpanzee in getting used to a stimulus. Much of a wild gorilla's mental ability, however, appear to be focused on feeding.

Programs for foraging

Mountain gorillas do not seem to need much brain power. They are surrounded by food and have little to worry about besides settling the occasional squabble or fighting off a predator or rival. Is there more to the gorilla than this?

Gorillas have a kind of ecological intelligence that they use to find food. There is evidence that they can appreciate the passing of the seasons and anticipate when particular foods, such as a favorite fruit or patch of bamboo, are ripening or sprouting and are ready to be harvested. Silver-backs have been seen to make a beeline for certain trees before any other group can take possession of them. The lowland gorilla is mainly a fruit eater, but the mountain gorilla cannot rely on fruit as a source of food and must turn to what is available in the alpine moss forests and temperate meadows. It eats the leaves and pithy stems of herbaceous plants, a diet that is nutritionally superior to fleshy fruit because it is rich in protein and trace elements. Many of the plants in the Virunga mountains, however, are protected by spines, stings, and hooks, or encased in hard indigestible tissues, and therefore difficult to eat. Foliage like this is usually consumed by cattle, deer, and antelope since these animals have specialized stomachs and intestines

 HUMAN DANGER

One of the biggest threats to the gorilla family is from the destruction of their habitat by a rapidly expanding human population. Agriculture and logging are clearing ever larger areas of forest. There is an inevitable loss of living space, but there are other dangers, too. Gorillas are killed, for example, when they raid crops. Above all, there is the bush-meat trade, in which gorilla and other wild meats are eaten locally or sold on. This is now widely seen as the most serious threat to the gorillas' survival in the wild. Body parts are also used for amulets to guard against disease or traded as souvenirs to tourists. In southern Cameroon, gorilla hair is believed to protect a person against spells, and tying a gorilla's finger or toe to a pregnant woman is thought to ensure that her offspring will be healthy. Gorillas confront danger with a display of size, strength, and bluff. A silverback will stand and try to intimidate an opponent by showing his chest, thus providing a hunter's rifle with an easy target.

The hands of a silverback are sold in a central African bazaar.

1

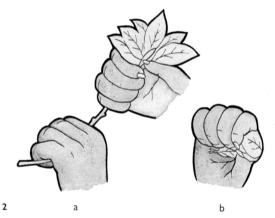

2   a   b

1. A mountain gorilla holds a plant stem. The thumb is smaller than a human's.

2. A gorilla eats nettles by stripping the leaves off the stem (a) and later folding them into a parcel (b).

3. Sometimes gorillas bring objects to their nose or mouth to check them.

filled with a gut flora that breaks down plant cellulose in order to get at the nutrients inside. Gorillas deal with vegetation in another way, by using their hands.

Two common foods for gorillas are nettles, which have painful stings, and a vine known as bedstraw, which is covered in tiny climbing hooks. During the course of a meal, the gorilla must be capable of precise and well-coordinated manual movements in order not to be stung or injured by the plants' defenses. The most unpleasant stings of nettles are found on the main stem, leaf petiole, and along the edge of the leaf blade, so the gorilla must deal with these before putting the leaves anywhere near its sensitive lips. The simplest way would be to pick up leaves one by one, hold each one by the petiole, and nibble at the leaf blade, but this would be an inefficient way of feeding. Instead, the gorilla has figured out a way to maximize each mouthful. It grabs the base of the main stem, and at the same time shapes its hand into a cone shape. It sweeps its hand up, stripping a whorl of leaves off the stem. It repeats the movement several times while holding the already stripped whorls in the lower fingers until it has a good handful of leaves. The gorilla then holds the leaf blades in one hand, grabs the leaf stems in the other, and twists both hands until the petioles come off of the leaves. The petioles are thrown away and the leaves are ready for the next part of the process. Any dead leaves or other debris are picked out carefully, but the gorilla must still deal with the stings at the edges of the leaves. It does this by taking a handful of leaves and folding them over its thumb to form a parcel with the

3

stings inside and the underside of the leaf, which is relatively sting free, on the outside. The parcel of leaves is then popped into the mouth.

The vine presents another problem. The tiny hooks could catch in the throat and cause the gorilla to choke. However, it chooses the tender, green stems and gathers them in one hand, while adding to the bundle with the other hand, much like somebody gathering a bunch of flowers. Dead leaves are removed meticulously, after which the bundle is rolled against the chin and then cut by

slicing bites using the cheek teeth, much like somebody chopping herbs.

A learning process

Researchers know that the complicated ways in which gorillas deal with their difficult foods is learned behavior, and that far from being an automatic process, it is under voluntary control. The fact that a gorilla can go back and add to its handful of nettles or bundle of vine means ▷▷

1. A field researcher working with a "habituated" group of mountain gorillas is able to observe their behavior from up close.

2. (opposite) A three-year-old lowland gorilla at an animal orphanage in Brazzaville treats its keeper as an honorary gorilla.

 CONSERVATION AND RESEARCH

In the wild, gorillas are threatened by destruction of their forest home, the bush-meat trade, and by the ravages of wars. Several wildlife charity organizations, such as the Dian Fossey Gorilla Fund and the International Gorilla Conservation Program of the Africa Wildlife Foundation, are supporting research and active conservation in the field (see p. 94 for the websites of these and the other organizations mentioned here). Despite the attention, the gorilla is listed as "threatened with extinction" in CITES (Convention on International Trade in Endangered Species), and as "endangered" in the Red Data Book of the IUCN (The World Conservation Union). Populations in Equatorial Guinea and Nigeria are considered "critically endangered". There are many scientists, conservationists and ordinary individuals who are trying to ensure that the gorilla never has to be listed as "extinct."

The grave of Dian Fossey lies near those of mountain gorillas killed by poachers.

1. Mountain gorillas sometimes feed on crops from farms adjacent to their national park. Some are killed as a result.

2. Park rangers carry the body of a mountain gorilla killed by poachers. With many wars in the area, gorillas are also killed for bush meat to feed people displaced by the conflicts.

that it is keeping track of the process and knows exactly where it is in the cycle. If it did not, it might become confused, say, when it stops to clean out inedible debris, and might start to roll a nettle, instead of a vine, against its chin. Gorillas are brighter than this.

The learning process starts when the gorilla is an infant. From the day it is born, a youngster is showered by plant debris when its mother is feeding, and when it can start to investigate the world for itself, inevitably it will begin to recognize the plants in the forest. Then, all it has to do is learn the elaborate sequence of events that enables it to convert a nettle leaf or a vine stem into food. A young gorilla learns quickly, even before it is weaned at around three years old, and its teacher must be either its mother, which it accompanies everywhere, or the silverback, the only other member of the group with which it is likely to have any meaningful contact at mealtimes. Other members of the group would not tolerate the presence of the infant or its mother when feeding, and they would be hidden behind foliage anyway. Probably, the infant learns the general technique from its mother by imitation and then the fine detail is added by trial and error, both mani-festations of intelligence. It means that a young gorilla faced with a juicy blackberry on a prickly stem will have learned how to strip the blackberry fruits and leaves delicately from the prickly stem by stretching back its lips and using only its front incisor teeth. Gorillas are clearly more intelligent than they at first appear.

2

LANGUAGE

While it is difficult to test gorillas in the wild for signs of intelligent behavior, those in captivity may give us a window into the gorilla's mind. To do this, gorillas are taught a special language. Gorillas have a vocal apparatus that is incapable of human speech, but they have been taught sign language. The star pupil is Koko, a female lowland gorilla who now lives in the Gorilla Foundation research facility in northern California. Her teacher is signing pioneer Francine (Penny) Patterson, who has lived with Koko for most of the gorilla's life. Koko has been taught how to use American   ▷▷

If a wild gorilla infant loses its mother, it stops playing, loses its appetite, and falls into a deep depression that may last for a year.

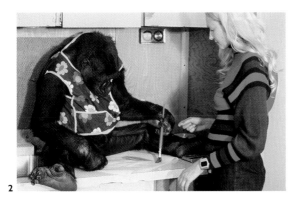

2

3

▷ USING TOOLS

Gorillas are not tool users like chimpanzees and orangutans, although they do use simple weapons, such as vegetation, which they throw at intruders. However, this is not necessarily an indication of lower intelligence. As contented and well-fed vegetarians, gorillas do not need tools, yet in captivity they can be taught to use all sorts of tools to solve problems. In an experiment with a young (15–38 months old) lowland gorilla and a macaque, the two animals were able to use string to drag objects and sticks to manipulate them. The macaque did this in a random fashion, where the gorilla showed itself to be more flexible at solving any problem given to it. In another experiment, gorillas, orangutans, and gibbons were tested to see which hand they used the most when unfastening a clasp or retrieving an object. The orangutans used both hands equally, the gibbons were mainly left handed, and the gorillas were right handed. Captive gorillas are accomplished artists. They will paint pictures, especially with bright poster paint, and work with unexpected concentration. They will even get upset if interrupted and seem to know when they have finished. They rip off a page to start another one.

1. (opposite) Koko "writing" with pen and clipboard. The tongue protruding between her lips is a sign of concentration seen in wild gorillas, too.

2. Koko had already taken to painting when she was young. Here she is concentrating hard on the task in hand.

3. Koko's paintings offer intriguing glimpses into her mind and feelings.

▷ THE MIRROR TEST

Apes are generally considered to be more intelligent than monkeys, but is this really true? What exactly is it that apes can do that monkeys cannot? Apes and monkeys have been tested to see if they can identify themselves. This is done by painting a mark on the face or a part of the body that the animal can see only by looking at itself in a mirror. If it recognizes that the spot is on itself and tries to remove it, it is deemed to have passed the "mirror test." Monkeys do not appear to recognize themselves, and will often go behind the mirror looking for the "other" monkey. Chimpanzees and orangutans, by contrast, are capable of self recognition and can be seen to concentrate as they try to remove the mark. For her part, Koko also passes the test. Like the other great apes, gorillas are capable of self recognition.

3

sign language for the deaf in order to communicate with her teachers. She has learned a vocabulary of several hundred signs and can string together simple words and phrases. How much of this does she understand and how linguistically able is she? Is her performance simply mimicry or is she actually learning how to communicate with humans using a convenient interface between gorillas and humans?

The jury is still out on how we should interpret sign-language research, but the achievements of Koko and her gorilla companion Michael are nothing short of remarkable. Koko was quick to pick up sign language, and her first signs were "drink," "food," and "more," things dear to a gorilla's heart. She then began to sign two-word combinations. A mixture of cereal and milk, for example, was signed as "food drink." The next great leap forward was when Koko asked questions, cocking her head and holding eye contact at first to change a statement into a question. On one occasion a woodpecker was drumming outside and her teacher signed "Koko, listen bird." Looking into her teacher's eyes, Koko signed "bird" and raised her eyebrows, changing "bird" into "bird?".

Koko's working vocabulary includes signs for "belly button," "friend," "lollipop," "airplane," and "stethoscope." She plays with dolls and looks at picture books, signing to herself and naming things, but like a human child, she does not like people watching her while she plays. Koko can be devious and lie, attempting to shift the blame from herself to one of her teachers for a misdemeanor, such as breaking a sink. She has also learned how to trade insults, using "swear" words such as "dirty"

1. Baby Koko is learning the sign for "more" from her teacher Dr. Patterson.

2. As a young gorilla, Koko was afraid when taunted in play by plastic toy alligators. She has overcome that fear and now often uses a tiny rubber alligator to "scare" her human friends.

3. Koko has become a celebrity among gorillas, and the research institute raises funds with her image as dolls and cardboard cutouts. The work continues. Koko now has a computerized "voice" that speaks the words associated with an on-screen icon that she touches.

1

2

1. Ecotourists in the Virunga mountains are allowed to watch groups of mountain gorillas that are accustomed to humans.

2. A park ranger dismantles a poacher's snare. The snare is put out to catch antelope, but often they entrap gorillas by their hands or legs.

3. A field researcher is allowed into the gorilla's world, but for how much longer will they be found in the wild?

Following page: If gorillas continue to be killed by humans, then the only place we might see them in the future is in zoos.

and "toilet," and she can be ironic. She was once asked to make the sign for "drink" but refused to do it, even though she had done it many times before. The teacher finally pleaded with Koko and, sitting back nonchalantly and grinning, she finally signed a perfect "drink," not to her mouth but to her ear.

Why a gorilla should pick up and perform sign language in this way is unclear. It was once generally believed that in their natural environment gorillas are no more than the primate equivalent of cows, with no need to consider the future as, for example, a cooperative hunter might have to do. Cooperation needs some planning and even discussion, no matter how simple.

It is clear, though, that gorillas in the wild excel at all sorts of social skills. They have long-lived social groups and need to function effectively in small, close-knit units. This has resulted in the evolution of an increased brain size. The ability to "think ahead" could be important when amalgamating the conflicting pressures of competition and cooperation that exist in a group of mainly unrelated females.

In fact, gorillas in the wild have their own "language" of gestures and vocalizations that are clearly important in a close society. It could be this social need that allows the gorilla to do things such as speak to us in a sign language in the language-rich captive environment. In view of the way we have treated gorillas since their discovery in 1847, however, if a wild gorilla is ever taught sign language, one wonders what it would say to us.

3

▷ GORILLAS UNDER THREAT

For some endangered species, such as the golden lion tamarin, zoological gardens and research institutions have become a last refuge. Captive breeding and reintroduction programes have been the last-ditch effort in preventing species from going extinct. Gorillas are not yet in this state, but zoos worldwide are making sure there is a viable captive-breeding program as an insurance policy if the worst should happen. In Africa, meanwhile, wildlife organizations have programs to teach local people the importance of ensuring the survival of gorillas and their habitat.

A conservation film shown in Rwanda.

FURTHER INFORMATION

BOOKS

A. F. Dixson, *The Natural History of the Gorilla* (Weidenfield and Nicolson, 1981)
A volume in The World Naturalist series giving an overview of gorilla research in the 1980s, both in the wild and in captivity.

Dian Fossey, *Gorillas in the Mist* (Hodder and Stoughton, 1983)
A detailed account of Dian Fossey's observations of mountain gorillas in the Virunga Mountains, Rwanda, before her tragic death.

Francine Patterson and Eugene Linden, *The Education of Koko* (Andre Deutsch, 1982)
A fascinating and sometimes moving chronicle of the early days of Patterson's experiment to teach sign language to a gorilla.

Ian Redmond, Eyewitness Guides: *Gorilla* (Dorling Kindersley, 1999)
An authoritative and popular children's book featuring gorillas and other primates.

George Schaller, *The Mountain Gorilla* (University of Chicago Press, 1963)
An account of Schaller's pioneering work with mountain gorillas in the Parc des Virungas, Congo.

MAGAZINE

BBC Wildlife Magazine
A monthly look at wildlife and conservation world wide.

WEBSITES

America Society of Primatologists
http://www.asp.org

Convention on International Trade in Endangered Species (CITES)
http://www.international.fws.gov/global/cities

Dian Fossey Gorilla Fund
http://www.gorilla-fund.org
http://www.dianfossey.org

Fauna and Flora International
http://www.ffi.org.uk

International Gorilla Conservation Program of the Africa Wildlife Foundation
http://www.awf.org

International Primate Protection League
http://www.ippl.org/index.html

International Primatological Society
http://indri.primate.wisc.edu/pin/ips.html

Primate Conservation
http://www.primate.org

Primate Society of Great Britain
http://www.ana.ed.ac.uk/PSGB/home.html

The World Conservation Union (IUCN)
http://www.iucn.org

INDEX